A. M. Shade
301 Rolling Ridge Dr.,
State College, PA 16801

W9-DEW-452

A book of COMFORT

To help and inspire in troubled times

DR R BRASCH

ANGUS
& ROBERTSON

An imprint of HarperCollins*Publishers*

Scripture quotations are from The New King James Version,
Copyright © 1982 by Thomas Nelson Inc.
Used by permission.

All efforts have been made to contact the copyright
owners of the material in this book. Where this has
not been possible, the Publishers invite the persons
concerned to contact them.

AN ANGUS & ROBERTSON BOOK
An imprint of HarperCollinsPublishers

First published in Australia in 1991
Reprinted in 1991
CollinsAngus&Robertson Publishers Pty Limited (ACN 009 913 517)
A division of HarperCollinsPublishers (Australia) Pty Limited
4 Eden Park, 31 Waterloo Road, North Ryde, NSW 2113, Australia

HarperCollinsPublishers (New Zealand) Limited
31 View Road, Glenfield, Auckland 10, New Zealand

HarperCollinsPublishers Limited
77– 85 Fulham Palace Road, London W6 8JB, United Kingdom

Text copyright © R. Brasch 1991

This book is copyright.
Apart from any fair dealing for the purposes of private study,
research, criticism or review, as permitted under the Copyright Act,
no part may be reproduced by any process without written
permission. Inquiries should be addressed to the publishers.

National Library of Australia
Cataloguing-in-Publication data:

Brasch, R. (Rudolph), 1912–
    A book of comfort.

    ISBN 0 207 17094 0.

    1. Bereavement – Literary collections.

    2. Grief – Literary collections. 3. Death –

    Literary collections. I. Title.

820. 8353

Illustrations by Megan Smith
Typeset in 9/13 pt Palatino
Printed in Hong Kong

5   4   3   2
95 94 93 92 91

Preface

A Book of Comfort is a source of inspiration for all those who are facing troubled times. It offers compassion and understanding in moments of sorrow and its message of optimism makes it a thoughtful gift for a friend or family member – or for yourself.

No one is alone in their misfortune. Whether suffering through separation, the loss of a loved one, disappointment, sickness, guilt or the traumas of retirement and old age, share the thoughts of others who have also faced uncertainty in their lives and ask the same questions. Why do we suffer? Why is there death? Why must the innocent experience pain?

A Book of Comfort uses poetry and legends, sayings and anecdotes, prayers and passages from the Bible to suggest ways of rebuilding life with courage and dignity. Its gentle words of wisdom will give hope for the future. As British Prime Minister Benjamin Disraeli once said 'Life is too short to be little'.

Dedicated

to

_____

_____

Your own thoughts and feelings may be expressed here
and such words, dates and recollections as you wish to
record year by year.

In the walk of life, I
have fallen many times.
Only the belief that God will
forgive me has helped me
get up and go on — knowing
full well that I will most
likely fall again.

CONTENTS

This time, like all other times, is a very good one, if we but know what to do with it.

RALPH WALDO EMERSON

STRENGTH FOR THE FUTURE

'What is life's heaviest burden?' a youth asked. 'To have nothing to carry – because it atrophies all your strength', was the reply.

The power of optimism

When all seems to have gone wrong, we must stay optimistic. This does not mean we foolishly blind our eyes to facts. Mature optimism recognises things as they are. It does not diminish the difficulties we confront, but it refuses to succumb to them or to see any reason to give up or give in.

Nelson lost an eye, Beethoven turned deaf, and Robert Louis Stevenson contracted tuberculosis. But none of them gave up the fight. Misfortune never touched their hearts. They never thought of saying, 'I've had it!' In fact their greatest achievements were yet to come.

The Past is for Wisdom
The present for Action
The Future for Joy.

<small>AUTHOR UNKNOWN</small>

H o p e

Two men looked out of the prison bars;
The one saw mud; the other the stars.

FREDERICK LANGBRIDGE

A person can live several weeks without food and days without water but never without hope. Because people had hope in their hearts, no drought, flood, earthquake or bad season could stop them from returning to their homes, farmsteads and fields – to rebuild and replant.

In his search for a new source of natural rubber in plant matter, Thomas Edison made numerous experiments. But each in turn proved unsuccessful. After his 50 000th failure, a discouraged assistant said to him, 'Mr Edison, we have made 50 000 experiments and have had no results'. 'Results!' exclaimed the great inventor with enthusiasm, 'we have wonderful results. We now know 50 000 things which won't work. Let's go on with the next experiment!'

Conflicts would have ended in catastrophe without the hope of state leaders who, against all odds, persevered to pursue peace.

Patients in intensive care could never go on fighting for life if they did not have hope. It keeps them going.

Hope brings religious people to their churches, synagogues, mosques and temples in search of God's help. Without hope women and men are doomed to despair, frustration and defeat. There is plenty of reason for hope, if you will only look for it.
Sorrow is like a toothache in your heart.

HEINRICH HEINE

FOR THOSE WHO ARE HURTING

Many and diverse are those trying and unfortunate life situations most of us have to face at one time or another. They include the failure of a business venture, disappointment of many kinds, the breaking up of a marriage, children leaving home, the traumas of retirement and old age, irreversible illness and terminal sickness. Added to these are day-to-day frustrations, having to look after someone very close to us who is chronically sick and, saddest of all, the loss of a loved one.

We ask many questions and ponder over possible answers. What is the meaning of it all? What should I do? What is the significance of death?

But we are also aware that all these experiences, though of the most personal nature, are universal. There is no-one on earth who has not at some time faced the uncertainties of life, as well as bereavement, and not asked the same questions.

Some of the thoughts of others on the very questions you are now considering may help you. They may be like voices calling you out of darkness to paths unknown, yet paths of comfort and peace.

Estrangement

Through an accumulation of minor circumstances (possibly beyond your control) or even without realising that it was happening, a closeness you had to someone really dear, is lost. The very person with whom you were on such intimate terms, now is like a stranger. A wall stands between you.

Perhaps you have outgrown your relationship. Your interests might have changed. Assess the situation rationally and unemotionally. Talk it out with each other – without allotting blame. Try to re-establish communications. Be prepared to make concessions.

If all this fails, accept reality and do so without rancour. Agree that each of you go your separate ways, yet be grateful for the time of your mutual concern, even though it did not last. After all, it contributed to your happiness and enriched your life at least part of the way.

D i v o r c e

If all attempts at reconciliation have failed and divorce has become necessary, it must not be looked upon as a disaster. Accept the inevitable in dignity and without bitterness.

Divorce is a kind of bereavement, a loss of good times, shared joys, goals and aspirations. Its danger is that it may result in feelings of anger or guilt. It may lead to loneliness, by either withdrawing from former friends, or being shunned by them and then to bitterness and cynicism about all members of the opposite sex. Wisely and calmly face these possibilities and be determined not to become their victim. Everyone going through the identical crisis has to learn to surmount it.

Part in amity and not in anger. Do not bear grudges or harp on things that went wrong. Avoid dwelling on past hurts, quarrels and miseries, or blaming yourself or your former partner.

Establish a new life, regarding your marital break-up as an unfortunate experience of your life which you just could not escape, and as a hard lesson. Never indulge in self-righteousness and self-pity nor in self-accusation. Beware of the hazard of loathing marriage altogether and becoming too wary or frightened ever again to seek out another spouse.

However difficult it may seem at first, stay friends with your ex-partner, now that you go your separate ways. Relate to each other positively and do not forget that once you did love each other deeply and shared many happy days, though they did not last.

If there are children, do not involve them or try to make them see your side of the story. Do not try to buy their affection with presents or special treats. They are the children of both of you and therefore should be your common concern, lest they suffer by your default. In spite of your parting, they remain your link. They must never become the debris of your shattered marriage. They are a legacy of your former love of which you both should have reason to be proud for ever.

God grant me serenity to accept the things I cannot change, courage to change the things I can, and wisdom to know the difference.

The art of being wise is the art of knowing what to overlook.

WILLIAM JAMES

Miscarriage and infant death

It is the most trying time for a couple when the joy of birth or its very anticipation turns into tragedy. For parents to lose an infant after the short time they were blessed with it is traumatic.

Truly to understand it, is beyond human ken. Maybe great suffering or disfigurement in mind or body was spared to the life that never was. Perhaps the loss is a test of strength. God would not have placed the burden upon you if He had not known that you would be strong enough to bear it. But trying to reason it out will only increase your agony.

You must accept the loss as one of the sad mysteries of life. Learn to cope with it by including it as part of your life and talking about it. By sharing and expressing your feelings and thoughts with your partner, you will become even closer to each other and further deepen your mutual love. Remember as well that you now possess a great gift: the ability to bring comfort to others who have suffered a loss like yours.

Sickness

Take your sickness as a test. You can discover values
denied to others and prove your mental and emotional
armour. Find something to occupy you positively and
regard your present condition like passing through a dark
tunnel – with bright sunlight waiting for you outside.
Make the most of every moment.

Looking after
the chronically ill

Caring for the chronically ill is a most dedicated pursuit.
It is very hard indeed on those who have a loved one to
look after, day in and day out, almost without respite. It is
not made easier if the need for continuous attention
means being housebound almost all the time.

If such is your fate, bear it with fortitude, without
becoming frustrated or even losing patience. It will make
your life meaningful in a way never expected. No-one
could ever fulfil a nobler task. The knowledge that you
ease the heavy burden of one you love, will give you extra
power and the comfort you need so much.

A husband looking after his chronically ill wife, regarded
it a labour of love. It never tired or depressed him. He felt,
'it is a God-given ministry.' Whenever things seem to get
you down, remember his words and you will find
renewed strength to carry on.

Coping with serious illness

If you learn that you or a loved one is suffering from a serious illness, do not give up hope. A doctor's diagnosis can only establish facts as they are at the moment. Remissions are known to have occurred, at times inexplicably and, with the constant advance of technology and science, new drugs, skills and treatments are continually being introduced with formerly undreamt of results. They may dramatically change a so far medically desperate problem into a situation of hope. Whatever the prognosis, it is not final and many useful and happy years may still be ahead.

Great (and often unrecognised) is the power of the mind over the body. We carry within us resources of unknown strength which have never been used. This is the moment to draw on them and to realise their potential. Although at times you might rebel against God and ask, 'What are you doing to me?', faith will enable you and your dear ones to endure what cannot be understood. For a religious person, prayer will bring fortitude and acceptance. However, all individuals have their own way of responding and should do so calmly and courageously.

Caring decisions

One of the great and often unexpected tragedies of life is when someone dear and near to us has to be 'institutionalised'. The very term horrifies us. Even in our enlightened age, some foolishly still consider mental illness as a stigma. It is no different from any other sickness which necessitates hospitalisation.

Those who are mentally impaired are not bereft of joy. The ultimate value of their lives is merely different from ours and they may possess precious gifts we ourselves lack. Every life is sacred and its dimensions extend far beyond our mind's vision and comprehension. In fact, anyone so afflicted is entitled to more protection and reverence than the 'normal' person, not less.

When it becomes essential to seek alternative accommodation for a person, the intention is not to isolate or to hide their existence. It is for their own good and therefore nothing to be ashamed of or to be kept a secret. Mental hospitals, group homes and halfway houses offer an opportunity to those thus stricken to enjoy their own quality of life and, strange though it may sound, happiness of a different kind.

They are looked after with understanding and care by highly qualified staff and although it may not be generally known, 'institutionalised' people do not feel outcast or forsaken. On the contrary they are happier among their peers than they would be within their family. You will surely miss your dear one, but you will wisely acknowledge and appreciate that they feel safe and are properly looked after.

Letting go

Seeing one's family grow up is one of the joys of parenthood. Children fill the home with laughter and mirth – in spite of the problems which are part of the process of their gaining maturity.

Then the day comes when your children leave home. At times you may even feel that they could have stayed on a little longer. Suddenly your entire existence is changed. The house seems so empty. You become lonely and depressed.

There is no reason for such a negative attitude. In fact, you should be happy for your children to have reached this stage, to see them find their own feet and take up the challenges of life. It should be a source of pride to see your children become independent and assume a meaningful identity in the adult world.

Recognise the benefit of such a move for you as parents as well. It provides you with a new beginning. Once again you can give all your time to each other and follow pursuits not previously possible because of your parental duties and responsibilities.

Thus the new situation will prove not a loss but rewarding for all concerned. You will look forward to frequent reunions, not merely in the way of parents and children now, but as close friends in a totally novel kind of affectionate and meaningful companionship.

Business failure

Failure is not falling down. It is remaining there when you have fallen.

SIR ABE BAILEY

Business failure is not the end of the world. Don't sit among the ruins and be discouraged. However paradoxical it may sound, you can develop success out of a failure.

Every venture has its occasional setback. It is the risk you take and wisely you have to accept the consequences and learn from them. Make a new plan at once and follow it through.

Make an inventory of your assets – and not merely the material ones. You must have had the ability in the first place to start and build up what you have now lost. You still have your brain power. You still have your health. You still have a loving family who will support you in your new enterprise. Whatever your new undertaking may be, embark on it with an adventurous spirit, with enthusiasm and optimism.

Nothing in life is free. Sooner or later everything has to be paid for. The experience of your failure was the price you had to pay for your future success.

Failure is the line of least persistence. It has been said that people begin their success where others end in failure.

Retirement

The worst reaction to being retired is to feel a 'has-been'. Nothing could be more devastating. Those who have filled a leading position and have to watch how loyalties and friendships are quickly being switched to their successor, may well be reminded of the old saying, so true not only of royalty but of life itself, 'The King is dead. Long live the King'.

Accept retirement as an event in the chronology of your life. In the way present-day society is organised it tries to make room for those who follow and, understandably from their point of view, are not prepared to wait until you are dead.

Look at retirement as a release from day-to-day responsibilities. Now you are free to take up a new role, do what you like best and mix with whoever you choose.

Confront the fact of retirement gracefully and not with resentment. Otherwise, you will not only be miserable for the rest of your life but, worse still, you will destroy the happiness of your spouse who stood by you supportively and encouragingly throughout the many years of your sometimes trying duties.

Having served in a special capacity for so considerable a time, there will be few who equal your experience, and many people or organisations will appreciate your advice.

Don't cease to be active. You now have the opportunity to direct your energy and mind into new channels and to explore and expand like the retired executive who started to grow bonsai trees as a hobby. Soon some friends,

attracted by the plants' beauty, purchased a few and
before long, the retired executive
had established a thriving 'business'.

Retirement is only the end of one chapter and the
beginning of a new one. It should be spelled 're-tyre-
ment'. You put on a new tyre and become involved with
fulfilling new activities and relationships.

Some people misinterpret retirement as a loss of stature.
Others refuse to retire out of mere greediness. Nothing is
ever enough for them. They amass their first million and
fulfil their initial aim but do not stop there. They then
promise to retire 'when I have got my second million' but
keep on postponing until it is too late to enjoy their
wealth, as in the process of acquiring it, the stress ruined
their health. For them it is well to recall the story of
Pyrrhus and the sage. When Pyrrhus, the famous king of
Epirus, told the sage that he was about to conquer Sicily,
the sage asked Pyrrhus what he intended doing after that.
'Then I shall conquer Africa,' Pyrrhus replied. 'And after
that?', the wise man now wanted to know. 'Then I'm
going to conquer the world!' 'And then?', the sage further
inquired. 'Then' said Pyrrhus, 'I shall rest and be happy,'
to which the philosopher challenged him, 'Why not rest
and be happy now?'

Happiness is not something which other people bestow
on you. You yourself give – or deny – it. You do so not
least by the manner and use of your retirement. You may
be able to thank God for the fullness of your years and the
richness of your days.

14

Facing old age

The ageing process brings with it certain changes. Faculties slow down, names are forgotten and aches and pains, unknown before, come and go. All this is the price you pay for being fortunate enough to reach old age.

Whether it proves a burden or a blessing depends largely on your attitude. If you adopt the right perspective, you will not give disproportionate attention to losses and failures, the inevitable result of advancing years, and become preoccupied with your body.

You have every reason to be grateful to live at a time of phenomenal progress in treating geriatric disabilities. Many ailments which, not so long ago, proved beyond help, and deteriorations that could not be halted, are now conquered. This is something which might well happen with what is troubling you at present.

Make up your mind that you will have to live with certain conditions that are part of ageing and learn to adjust to them. Count your blessings and think of the people who are worse off than you. Cultivate new friends. Keep active and busy. Take up pursuits and hobbies that until now you have had no time for. Keep on having a future instead of merely a past.

You need not be counted among those of 'old age' but be admired as one 'well aged' and young at heart.

Losing a pet

Pets are the most wonderful friends. They truly share our joys and our sorrows and seem to sense when they are needed most. Good companions, at times they appear to understand us better than humans do.

But like all creatures, they have to die. We must accept the fact of their passing as inevitable and as part of the laws of nature. Their lifespan, if counted in years, is shorter than ours. It is important to remember that, with all the joy and love we received from them, we have given them the best of lives.

Only those who have had a pet can realise how much it hurts when the vet has to put a beautiful cat or a loyal dog to sleep. On occasions, you may even have (unjustified) feelings of guilt. We must understand that it is done to save the animal much suffering and that it will go to sleep peacefully, without pain.

ON DEATH

AND DYING

The loss of a loved one shocks and bewilders us. If they were advanced in years, we still feel they were not old enough to have died. But if they were young, we ask for the reason why they had to be snatched away before their personality had fulfilled its promise.

The trauma of grief is an experience we must all share sooner or later. It makes us feel at one. The words written here therefore are intended to help and comfort everyone suffering bereavement. Whatever your faith or philosophy of life, may you find the strength and comfort you need so much at this sad hour. May you feel that death is not the end but the opening of an unknown door. Everything that happens has a hidden meaning, even if it is beyond our understanding.

Your memories belong to you for ever. Your beloved has cast off the ephemeral, but their spirit of love is still with you. You can honour them by being courageous and not downcast. May your sorrow be softened and may you find consolation and peace of mind.

. . . .

It is one of the paradoxes of human existence that everyone wants to live long but no one wants to grow old. We almost expect those fortunate enough to be blessed with an abundance of years to go on living for ever. Therefore, when the moment of passing arrives, it still comes as a blow. Everyone's lifespan is limited even if it exceeds the biblical 'three score years and ten or, by reason of strength, four score years'.

Wisely we must be ready to accept death as a reality and, indeed, be grateful for the privilege of having enjoyed their company for so many years – far beyond the allotted time. If, on the other hand, death relieves suffering, we should thankfully acknowledge it. As life is a privilege, death is sometimes a blessing. Never abandon a rational approach to death.

Death is not extinguishing the light; it is putting out the lamp because the dawn has come.

RABINDRANATH TAGORE

. . . .

Our attitude towards dying and death must be based on faith and not on fear. As a mature person, show your inner strength by bearing courageously the burden laid upon you.

Words are inadequate to express your feelings. Life seems to have lost its meaning. But ask yourself: is that how your dear one would like to see you? They loved you so much that if they could speak to you they would say, 'Don't feel unhappy. Honour my memory by seeing life's beauty and sunshine even now. It is difficult indeed, and yet, it can be done. I want to see you happy.'

. . . .

Life must be lived forward, but can only be understood backward. Don't reckon the importance of life in years. An hour of a glorious life beautifully spent is worth more than scores of years wasted.

What is it you appreciated most about your loved one?
Surely not just the outward features, but the selfless
kindness, the beauty of the soul and the spirit of love that
filled their physical being.

The value of peoples' lives does not depend on what they
had, but on what they were. Their greatness is not related
to the number of years lived, but is the result of the
quality of their lives. 'Look not at the flask, but at what it
contains.'

. . . .

Death cannot kill that which never dies. Love once
bestowed on earth is immortal. It lives on always. The
empty chair is not really empty. Your loved one has not
gone. Their spirit is still with you sharing, though on a
higher plane, your joys and your sorrows.

. . . .

You have had many a dream. How did you realise that it
was 'only a dream'? It was by waking up. Could not life
also be merely a dream, and death not a falling asleep, but
an awakening to a greater reality and a more complete
consciousness?

. . . .

Modern science has shown the indestructibility of matter
and energy. Religion has always taught the
indestructibility of the spirit or soul.

. . . .

Eternal life is not just a life carried on endlessly. It is a different kind of existence freed from the anxieties and disappointments of this earth and from its trivia and irrelevancies. Eternal life is full of exultation and bliss.

. . . .

In your sadness, when all within is dark, try to focus your mind on the 'perfect days' you had the good fortune and blessing to share. Remember the joy they gave you, how they made you laugh together and feel so happy.

Those perfect days are treasures you carry with you. Death cannot wipe them out. They are the most wonderful legacy left to you. Be grateful for these precious gifts which nothing can take from you. In your confusion and feeling of unreality, they will prove a solace and a source of strength.

. . . .

When confronted with death, we often think that dying means pain and even agony. Yet in reality it is just a peaceful and painless gliding into a higher sphere of life. Like birth, death is a sleep and a forgetting. The last words of one of the great English surgeons, John Hunter, were, 'If I had strength enough to hold a pen, I would write how easy and pleasant a thing it is to die'.

. . . .

Don't let us be selfish in our grief. Self-pity helps no-one. In the hour of our bereavement let us beware of giving vent to primitive superstitions. True mourning is not a matter of outward action. It belongs to the heart. We honour the memory of our loved ones most by serene dignity and quiet thought.

. . . .

To contrast life with death is a fallacy. The correct antithesis is birth and death. Life is permanent. It precedes birth and goes on – enriched and ennobled – after death. Birth and death are just stages on the path of life.

. . . .

It is difficult, especially for children, to make sense of death. 'When I was a child,' a woman who had made her mark in the world recollects, 'my father told me that as roots were put into the earth and came up as beautiful plants, so when the body was placed in the earth after death, its spirit unfolded in all its glory, to go home to God'. A childish thought perhaps, which nevertheless suggests growth and renewed hope.

. . . .

In an interview on the occasion of his eightieth birthday, American author Robert Frost was asked what he considered the most important thing life had taught him. His answer was contained in three short words, 'It goes on.'

. . . .

Even if at moments of tribulation we may be tempted to say, 'This is the end', life still goes on. It always has and it always will.

FACING SORROW, FINDING PEACE

Tragic loss is a fact of life that no philosophy can obliterate. But even if answers fail us, we must respond to the blow that has struck. In doing so it is essential to realise the all-importance of what we do with what has happened to us.

There is many a pitfall we must avoid at all costs. Conversely, it is necessary for us to take up certain fundamental tasks, however hard they might seem, wisely, constructively and courageously, with dignity and without fear. In fact, we must do things we might think we cannot do.

Why?

People are always asking,'Why?' Why do we suffer? Why is there death? Why must the young die? Why must the innocent experience pain? Why does God permit it all?

We cannot answer these questions. They baffle us. We have to admit that they are beyond our capacity to understand. Since our minds are so limited, we can only see part of the truth. God sees the whole. Some day we may discover the answers to our persistent questioning.

We are like the pagan who, to be convinced of God's existence, demanded to see Him. He was asked to look into the sun and, of course, was blinded by its fierce light and could see nothing. Thus, if he was unable to see even one of the myriad of God's creations, how then could he expect to fathom God Himself?

Not to be able to give an answer at the present moment, however, does not mean that there is no answer. We are ignorant because of the limit of our vision. 'For my thoughts are not your thoughts neither are your ways my ways, says the Lord. For as the heavens are higher than the earth, so are my ways higher than your ways and my thoughts than your thoughts.' We human beings cannot comprehend the infinite with our finite minds. We can see only fragments of life, not the whole of it. Let us admit the limitations of our knowledge and, with aching heart, trust that ultimately there is an answer, though we do not know it yet.

Give vent to your feelings

The bitterness of loss is devastating. It is equally true that if a loved one dies, our own grief is always more severe than anyone else's. This is not selfish but natural. The very closeness of the departed makes it so. It is just as those falling in love are convinced that no other love could ever compare with theirs. To deny it, would be foolish.

Bereavement creates a deep festering wound that can drain our emotions and freeze our thoughts. Therefore, be not afraid to give vent to your feelings. Do not keep back your tears. Express and don't suppress your anguish. Talk about it to those nearest to you, whenever you feel the need.

The fallacy of finality

Courage is the thing; all goes if courage goes.

JAMES MATTHEW BARRIE

There is nothing more tragic in life than to imagine that all hope is lost. Those who think that they have come to the end of the road, that they can go no further and that there is no help and no way out, are mistaken.

God never closes all doors although, stunned by the blow that has struck us, it may seem to us so. If we persevere with courage and faith, we shall find that God never forsakes us.

Disraeli, one of Britain's great state leaders, once said that 'There is no education like adversity'. Indeed, it is a test, perhaps a crucible, but also a means to greater strength.

When troubles beset us on our way, it is so easy to despair and to believe that things have gone so far out of control that to tackle them is beyond our power.

We ought to remember that we are not the only ones to find ourselves at an apparent impasse. Just as a kite rises against the wind, even the worst of troubles can strengthen us. As thousands before us have met the identical fate and mastered it, so can we!

Don't feel guilty

It is a common phenomenon that when we lose someone we love dearly, we suffer feelings of guilt. We start reproaching ourselves for words left unsaid and acts of kindness left undone. We imagine that it is our fault that these 'might-have-beens' were never realised. We blame ourselves for not giving enough time, or sufficient thought or care. 'If only' we had not waited and postponed things. 'If only' we hadn't spoken harshly or acted meanly.

If you are accusing yourself in this way, you need to realise that this is part of everyone's grief. It belongs to the normal pattern of mourning. There is no reason for you to feel guilty. On the contrary, it is only because of your deep love for the one you lost that you harbour sad feelings, thereby unnecessarily adding to your burden. To suffer from such an unsound guilt complex can play havoc with your life and health; worse still, it can deprive those who need you most now, of your help.

The absurdity of self-reproach is demonstrated by a woman who blamed herself totally for her husband's death. Because he had felt unwell, she had made him see the doctor who diagnosed a serious illness and advised an operation. There were complications and the man died. The woman was convinced that it was all her fault. She firmly believed that if she had not sent her husband to the doctor, there would have been no operation and no death. She totally misinterpreted her deep concern and her wise counsel because of her depressed state of mind.

An antidote for sorrow

What often appears to be the end of the road is merely a bend. Under no circumstances indulge in self-pity. Don't sit around feeling sorry for yourself. The best antidote for sorrow is to get busy. Start on a job. Work off your sadness by some physical activity. The least you can do is to go for a strenuous walk. It will make you feel better.

The loss of someone and the resulting loneliness it creates, inevitably causes bouts of depression. They may strike you most frequently at festive seasons, when the rest of the world seems to be jolly and enjoying the company of friends, whilst you feel forsaken and forgotten. You will experience this even more on anniversaries you once shared with the departed in joy and gladness. It might hit you quite suddenly, prompted by a tune, a picture, an object. Draw up a list for those moments. Write down things that need doing and names of people you ought to visit. When depression sets in, get up and tackle those tasks.

Don't focus your mind on yourself. Concentrate and keep busy doing something for someone else who may well be so much worse off than you.

Don't spend time brooding over sorrow and mistakes. The only people who never make mistakes are those who never do anything. Don't live in the past. The past must be a springboard.

Don't be the one who never gets over things. Keep busy at something. A very busy person never has time to be unhappy.

Rebuilding life

It is like a nightmare. How you wish to wake up and find that all the horrendous agony was an illusion. You must accept reality and learn that you have to rebuild your life.

It is particularly difficult when you have to make decisions, especially for a wife who had always depended on her husband's guidance. She may have to decide whether to keep on the home or move into a smaller dwelling or evaluate financial investments. How often then she might say, 'If only he were here to tell me what to do'.

Yet another danger lurks for those rebuilding a shattered existence. Moments may occur when, absorbed in a new task, we might not think of our loved one for a little while or we may suddenly laugh. To forget, if only temporarily, someone who should be constantly and exclusively in our thoughts makes us feel disloyal. Realise that such 'forgetfulness' is not real. On the contrary, it is a sign of the healing process.

Sorrow is as much part of life as joy. By overcoming our grief, we can prove our faith in God and honour those we mourn by carrying on their lives, fulfilling their unrealised dreams and their still uncompleted tasks.

MEETING PROBLEMS
HEAD ON

Don't lock yourself out

If life knocks you, as inevitably it will, you might lose the will to make the best of things and use the shattered fragments to build up something entirely fresh.

Have you ever experienced the feeling of frustration when you left your house keys indoors or the car key in the ignition? Almost everyone has done so at some time or another. Wisely, you then find some way to get in. Likewise, in life, don't lock yourself out.

Perhaps the reversal or loss that you have suffered has been sent to give you a totally new start. You have so much within you that you don't even know about – resources and gifts and strength. This is the moment to realise them.

A balanced view

If you hold a small coin close to your eyes, it will obstruct your view. Only if you keep it at a proper distance, will you see things beyond and in their right proportion.

Whatever has happened to you at this moment, of necessity must look very large and obscure everything else. After some time, when you have reached a certain distance from it, it might appear not only small but trifling.

The agony of uncertainty

As you go through life, make this your goal:
Watch the doughnut and not the hole!

AUTHOR UNKNOWN

Life is full of uncertainties. They haunt us in so many ways. There is the agony of uncertainty, when we wait for the result of an examination – at school, at university or in the doctor's surgery. We wait anxiously for someone dear to return from the operating theatre and to hear the surgeon's verdict.

Our present-day world has added its own share of uncertainties. You have saved up for your old age, but will the money be worth anything when that time comes?

Even the choice of an occupation or profession has become a problem. It is hard to foresee whether what appears at the moment to be a most promising and 'up-to-date' career, might not become obsolete at the time of graduation.

Never let an uncertainty overwhelm you. Have faith in the good and in God.

Problems

No matter who you are and what you do, you are bound
to strike problems. Don't be overwhelmed by them,
however vast and trying they seem. Life is bigger than
today's problems. Nothing of substance has ever been
achieved without adversity, difficulty or pain.

An irritant, like a grain of sand, creates the pearl in the
oyster. The tremendous pressure by the earth above,
produces coal and diamonds. Those who pick roses feel
their thorns. Kites rise against the wind and not with it.
On the other hand, do not exaggerate a difficulty you
encounter. Insignificant troubles have spoilt many happy
days. It has been said that it is not the mountain ahead,
but the small pebble in a shoe, that has worn people out.

Losing confidence

Never say something cannot be done.

When Michelangelo was asked to decorate the walls of
the Sistine Chapel, he felt completely inadequate to
undertake the task. It seemed beyond his power as he had
never done anything like it before. However, realising that
a refusal on his part would carry dire consequences, he
embarked on it against his better judgement and created a
masterpiece which has inspired the world ever since.

Don't underestimate your own ability and gifts. Face up
to the difficulties that confront you and go ahead with
renewed faith in yourself. Significantly, the literal
meaning of the word confidence is 'with trust'.

At times of worry

Worry is a universal disease. Who of us has not worried at one time or another? But if we recollect some of the anxieties that almost drove us out of our mind, we often find that many of them never happened.

Try to remember what you were worried about only a year ago. The chances are that you, too, won't be able to do so, though at the time it not only spoiled your day, but also made others miserable who deserved better.

The cost of worry is high. There are definite ways to combat it. Worry distorts your thinking, destroys your peace of mind and saps your energy. Accept circumstances the way they are and then make the best of them.

Merely trying to suppress your worry will be ineffective. It will keep on plaguing you and eventually overshadow all your thoughts. Face it squarely. In the majority of cases, you will find how unfounded it is. Above all, don't cross the proverbial bridge until you get there.

If nevertheless your worry continues to trouble you, don't keep it to yourself. Share it with someone on whom you can rely and with whom you can talk things over. It is not just a cliché that 'a trouble shared is a trouble halved'.

An old preacher used to greet every day with this prayer: 'O Lord, help me to remember that nothing is going to happen to me today that You and I together can't handle'. With such faith we need never worry.

Overcoming disappointments

Fear not for the future; weep not for the past.

PERCY BYSSHE SHELLEY

Who of us has not had disappointments? People we trusted implicitly have let us down. Someone we regarded a true friend has turned out to be anything but a friend. People we had previously supported and encouraged have dismally failed us in a crisis situation of our own.

It is so all-important to overcome and disregard disappointments. Instead, remember the many acts of kindness you experienced, at times from sources and people least expected.

Recollect the many happy surprises you had in the past. There is more good in the world than bad. Why then dwell on and single out the negative and let it discolour your outlook on life and spoil its enjoyment. Things could have turned out much worse.

Not infrequently, initial disappointments in retrospect prove to have been of value and benefit. Emerson once defined a weed as 'a plant whose virtues have not yet been discovered'. We often look with so much regret and longing upon the door which has closed that we do not see the one (or even two) opening up for us. 'Go forward, do not be discouraged or afraid.'

In thinking of the journey through time to eternity, humankind's imagination was roused to picture in vivid form beautiful stories through which comforting and elevating truth shines. Legends and allegories have inspired many to high thinking and noble conduct. They speak from the heart to the heart.

A great artist was once asked the meaning of his painting. His answer was, 'It means whatever you find in it'. May your mind interpret the meaning of these stories and your heart sense their message.

True values

A prince of the East owned a most precious gem which he wanted to be taken to a distant part of his kingdom. He entrusted a friend, whom he knew to be reliable, to undertake the task. However, instead of informing the friend of the real value of the stone he had placed in a small container, the prince tried to mislead him, saying that it was merely a brass button with a large rhinestone and of sentimental value only.

Thus the friend set out on his mission. Things did not go as expected. On the way, he was attacked by robbers. They took away everything he had, including the small box with the 'worthless' object.

When he reported the loss to the prince, he did not expect the nobleman's reaction, who was beside himself with rage. His trusted friend should have made an attempt to defend the treasure, the prince stormed. 'Treasure? Did you expect me to put up a fight for a worthless piece of glass?' the friend asked. When the prince told him of the precious gem of irreplaceable value, the man said, 'If only you had told me so from the beginning. Surely, had I known, I would have defended your treasure with my life!'

Trust demands honesty. Unless we appreciate and share the true values of life – and do so from the very beginning – they will be taken from us.

Broken shells

In the garden of Johnny's home was a tree in whose branches birds had built a nest. He was thrilled when one day, climbing up, he found four eggs in it. Almost daily now, he visited the nest. Then the family went away for the school holidays.

The first thing Johnny did on their return was to climb the tree to look at *his* nest. He was most upset to find that all that was left of the eggs were empty, broken shells.

Sobbing, he ran to his father telling him how the eggs were ruined. 'No, my son,' his father told him, 'you are mistaken. The best parts were inside, and they have become beautiful birds which have flown away.'

Winged words

A wrong word spoken, unthinkingly perhaps, can destroy happiness. A famous statesman prided himself on his habit of talking haltingly because, as he said, it always gave him sufficient time to carefully consider what he was going to say next.

A woman called on her minister, deeply distressed. She had gone around spreading nasty rumours and now realised all the heartache she had caused. 'How I wish,' she said, 'that I had kept silent. If only I could retract my words!' She would do anything to make amends and to undo the harm.

The minister set her a peculiar task. She was to go to the market and buy a chicken. She was then to walk slowly home and on the way to pluck the bird. 'Don't worry about the feathers,' he said, 'just drop them as you go along'. Having done so, she was to come back to see him.

The woman was mystified. His counsel made no sense to her. It seemed so easy and odd a way to make amends. Nevertheless, she did as she had been told and returned to the minister. She informed him that she had completed the task. 'Far from it,' was the reply. 'Your real task is only about to commence. Now go out again and gather up all the feathers.' Both knew that this was impossible. And yet, it was a lesson she would always remember. It is so easy to be sorry after the event. Words spoken in haste, are like those feathers.

Footprints in the sand

One night a man had a dream. He dreamed he was walking along the beach with the Lord. Across the sky flashed scenes from his life. For each scene, he noticed two sets of footprints in the sand; one belonging to him, and the other to the Lord.

When the last scene of his life flashed before him, he looked back at the footprints in the sand. He noticed that many times along the path of his life there was only one set of footprints. He also noticed that it happened at the very lowest and saddest times in his life. This really bothered him and he questioned the Lord about it. 'Lord, you said that once I decided to follow you, you'd walk with me all the way. But I have noticed that during the most troublesome times in my life there is only one set of footprints. I don't understand why when I needed you most you would leave me.'

The Lord replied, 'My precious, precious child, I love you and I would never leave you. During your times of trial and suffering when you see only one set of footprints in the sand it was then that I carried you.'

Author Unknown

Everything has to be paid for

Many years ago, a legend tells, a wise old king summoned his advisers to give them a special task. They were to compile a work containing 'the wisdom of the ages'. It should serve as an inspiration to all future generations.

It took a long time to complete the task but finally the advisors presented the king with the result of their effort in twelve huge volumes. 'This is the wisdom of the ages,' they proclaimed.

The king thanked the authors for their tremendous amount of work. But he was not satisfied. It was much too long. He feared no-one would read it. Thus he asked the men to return to their desks and to condense the volumes.

When, eventually, they handed the king one single book, he still was not content. Even this was too long. The sages were asked to reduce it even further. First the one volume into one chapter, then the chapter into one page, into one paragraph and, finally, into one sentence. At last the king was happy. 'This, indeed,' he said, 'is the wisdom of the ages. Once people realise its truth, most of their problems will be solved.' Concise and to the point, the one sentence read: 'There is nothing for nothing!'

How much is it worth?

A severely wounded soldier had to be left behind in no-man's-land. At the time, his expectation of survival was almost nil.

A friend's request to be permitted to go back to him was rejected, as it was assumed that meanwhile the man would have died. But the soldier insisted, 'I must go, as I know he is still alive.' His superior officer argued that even if that were so at the moment, it was unlikely that he would survive much longer. 'I can't take a chance with your life as well,' he explained.

But, persevering in his request, the soldier was eventually granted permission. Crawling through the barbed wire and rubble, he finally reached his pal, who miraculously was still alive. With every possible effort, he dragged him towards the trenches, but before he could reach them, the man had succumbed to his wounds.

'You see what happened,' the officer remarked. 'Was it worth risking your life?' 'Yes, he died,' admitted the soldier, 'but he was still alive when I got to him. He recognised me and said, "I knew you'd come John, I knew you would come!"'

An action that apparently had failed to succeed and did not save the soldier's life, nevertheless had been worth all the risk taken. It made the man die in peace, happily knowing that his friend had not forsaken him. And that was worth everything. A seemingly futile action may prove to have a lasting effect and be of abiding value.

A matter for choice: the parable of the three apples

A father who wanted to test his three sons' attitude towards life and simultaneously teach them a lesson, gave each of them an apple, part of which was rotten. Their reactions differed from son to son.

One boy ate the entire apple, including its rotten part. When the second son saw that the apple was imperfect, he threw it away altogether. The third son, however, cut out its bad part, to enjoy the rest.

Simple in itself, the parable vividly pictures three types of people. There are those who, without giving it any thought, swallow everything: good and bad, beneficial and harmful. They do so because either they don't take the time or they lack the wisdom to learn to select. Another category of people jump to conclusions and give up the fight easily. Having experienced some sad moments in life or a tragedy, they condemn life altogether.

Certainly, the world is far from perfect, but there is a lot of good in it. We don't have to shut our eyes to what is evil in order to appreciate the good that exists and the joys life brings. It is better to look at the sunlight than the shadows.

Mature and wise people have learned the art of choosing. Like the third son, they select the good and reject only the bad. Once we acquire this attitude, it will stay with us and help us in making our existence truly worthwhile, enriching and meaningful.

T w o   j e w e l s

No-one is exempt from the experience of bereavement nor
the feeling of helplessness it creates. A story tells how
a famous second-century scholar had to face
this shattering blow.

One day, whilst instructing his students, he was unaware
that the worst fate any parent can suffer, had befallen him.
His two gifted sons had been killed. It was left to the
distraught mother to break the news to him on his return.
Even in her grief, as a woman of faith and deep love, she
did so wisely.

The moment her husband had arrived home, she
explained that she needed his counsel urgently. A long
time ago, she claimed, someone had entrusted two
precious jewels into her care. He had not come back and,
with the passing of years, she had begun to consider the
precious stones as hers. Now, suddenly, the real owner
had turned up to reclaim his property. 'Must I give back
those jewels?' she asked her husband.

Aghast, he wondered what had happened to his wife,
even to put such a question. Surely, there was no doubt.
'This is something you should never have asked,' he
reprimanded her. How could she hesitate for the slightest
moment to hand over the property to its rightful owner.

It was exactly what his wife had expected him to say. Silently she led him to their sons' room. He, who had devoted his entire life to making other people happy, leading them, as it were, to the heights of brilliant sunshine, now himself had to walk through the valley of the shadow of death. Having enlightened thousands and knowing so many explanations to the problems facing humankind almost daily, he himself was confronted by the great mystery of the Unknown. Breaking out in tears, he lamented, 'My sons, my sons, the light of my eyes!'

Though despondent and deeply grieved, his wife knew her duty. Out of the depth of her soul, she uttered words of immortal wisdom: 'Did you not teach me that we must return that which is entrusted to our keeping? Our sons, these two jewels, were not ours, but God's. The Lord gave, and the Lord has taken away. Blessed be the name of the Lord.'

The mustard seed

A grief-stricken woman who had lost her only son called on a wise man renowned for his wondrous deeds. She pleaded for his help in having the boy returned to her.

To her surprise, he agreed to do so. However, she had first to fulfil one condition. She had to bring him a mustard seed from a home that was entirely free from sorrow. And the mother set out on her task...

Many years passed, but she did not return. Then, one day, quite by chance, the sage met her. He could hardly recognise her because she seemed to have changed so much, looking now happy and content.

Greeting her, he could not restrain himself from asking why she had never kept her appointment. To begin with, it seemed as if she did not even realise to what he was referring. Then she explained what had happened.

In her search for the mustard seed, she had visited many homes. On each occasion, she had found them so burdened with sorrow and sadness that she could not walk out, but felt impelled to share the people's misfortune and help them in facing and overcoming it.

'Who better than I,' she said, 'could understand their heavy burden and their desperate need? Who then was more qualified than I to stay and offer my help?'

Thus she remained in each home as long as she could be of service. In this pursuit, she had forgotten all about the appointment.

POEMS OF

PROMISE

Poets are endowed with a strong imaginative faculty.
They see things, great and small, more vividly than
ordinary people. All human beings have had experiences
that have deeply stirred them. Most of us cannot put
those experiences into words, but poets can and their
words are so chosen and arranged that they enable us to
share their vision of the reality of life.

Poetry can enlarge our being. It can show us depths in
ourselves and sympathy for others of which we were not
aware before.

Poetry is said to be the sister of sorrow, and, as a sister
should, it whispers courage and hope and reveals to us
the beauty as well as the pain of the finite heart that
yearns.

'Tis easy enough to be pleasant
When life flows along like a song.
But the man worthwhile is the man who will smile
When everything goes dead wrong.

ELLA WHEELER WILCOX

We live in deeds, not years; in thought, not breaths;
In feelings, not in figures on a dial.
We should count time by heart-throbs. He most lives
Who thinks most, feels the noblest, acts the best.

PHILIP JAMES BAILEY

Remember me when I am gone away,
Gone far away into the silent land;
When you can no more hold me by the hand,
Nor I half turn to go, yet turning stay.
Remember me when no more day by day
You tell me of our future that you plann'd:
Only remember me; you understand
It will be late to counsel then or pray.
Yet if you should forget me for a while
And afterwards remember, do not grieve;
For if the darkness and corruption leave
A vestige of the thoughts that once I had,
Better by far you should forget and smile
Than that you should remember and be sad.

CHRISTINA G. ROSSETTI

Burn out, my life, burn quick,
Not much is left now of the wick.
Let there be light on my last day,
To point the way.
Don't flicker, life, burn clear.
Then like a spring-thought disappear.
I hate to stint! Life blaze away!
Let me have light at least one day.

ABRAHAM REISEN – TRANSLATED BY J. LEFTWICH

A curse called cancer

For Sue

They say that 'cancer is a way of life, not a way to die'
but the havoc it wrought in you often made me cry.
Inexorably, contemptuously it usurped your mortal form
though didn't break your spirit which ever was so warm.

For six long years so bravely
you struggled with serenity
suffering for your family
'gainst this terrible obscenity.

Only when absolutely certain
our girls now wished you peace
did you draw the final curtain
then from pain get just release.

As grapes left to wither and moulder on the vines
make the most intense and yet sweetest of wine
treasured by kith and kin long since the fruit has gone
so be it with you my love, now your earthly life is done.

RICHARD BRIGGS, NEW YEAR'S DAY, 1990 *

Sue passed away at the age of forty-three, after having
borne her sickness with deep serenity. Her husband wrote
this poem on the following New Year's Day when on
awakening a renewed sense of loneliness overcame him.
In his own words, 'I had been caught off guard' and
'writing this poem lifted my spirits no end'.

* *Reproduced with the permission of Richard Briggs.*

45

If I can stop one heart from breaking,
I shall not live in vain;
If I can ease one life the aching,
Or cool one pain,
Or help one fainting robin
Unto his nest again,
I shall not live in vain.

EMILY DICKINSON

Money lost, little lost,
Honour lost, much lost,
Heart lost, all lost.

AUTHOR UNKNOWN

Not 'till the loom is silent
And the shuttles cease to fly,
Shall He unroll the canvass
And explain the reason why
The dark threads are as needful
In the Weaver's skillful hand
As the threads of gold and silver
In the pattern He had planned.

AUTHOR UNKNOWN

Keep on looking for the bright, bright skies;
Keep on hoping that the sun will rise;
Keep on singing when the whole world sighs,
And You'll get there in the morning.

A SONG

INSPIRATION THROUGH PRAYER

Prayer brings us in contact with God who fills the Universe with the spirit of love. We need love to soften our grief. We pour out our hearts to God.

As Elijah cried to God in his loneliness and felt again the power to go on, so may we be lifted by our prayers, from our confusion and feeling of abandonment to a calm acceptance of reality.

'I have been driven many times to my knees,' said Abraham Lincoln, 'by the overwhelming conviction that I had nowhere else to go. My own wisdom and that of all about me seemed insufficient for that day.'

Without using any prepared text, you may also express – quite spontaneously and in your own words – what your heart prompts you to say.

. . . .

I will lift up mine eyes unto the mountains;
From whence shall my help come?
My help cometh from the Lord,
Who made heaven and earth.

He will not suffer thy foot to be moved;
He that keepeth thee will not slumber.
Behold, He that keepeth Israel
Doth neither slumber nor sleep.

The Lord is thy keeper;
The Lord is thy shade upon thy right hand.
The sun shall not smite thee by day,
Nor the moon by night.

The Lord shall keep thee from all evil;
He shall keep thy soul.
The Lord shall guard thy going out and thy coming in,
From this time forth and for ever.

PSALM 121

. . . .

You who are all spirit give of your spirit unto man. The soul is yours and comes from you. By its presence our being is sanctified and life is hallowed. By its power man triumphs over the distresses of life and the darkness of the grave. For it partakes of your eternity. Help us, our God, to be worthy of our divine heritage.

Amen

. . . .

O Lord, my life seems dull and sad. I look ahead and see no hope. The dear one about whom my life turned is gone and is hidden from my sight. Give me courage to live my life alone and use it faithfully in your service and in helping others.

I recall incidents in the life which is just ended. I remember our effortless companionship, our sharing of everything: the sympathy, the help and the encouragement upon which I could always rely.

Is it all over? I look around and feel bewildered. I cannot believe my own loneliness. I imagine every moment I shall be roused from my terrible dream. Then again comes the dull sense of reality. O Lord, have pity on me! Fill my soul with comfort. Look upon my suffering and let me find peace. It is love which makes life beautiful, human love, the reflection of the divine. It is for this we strive, it is this which leads us unto you.

Almighty Father,
Help me in my sadness and my loneliness, for I need you
so. My beloved has gone from me and I am overwhelmed
with grief. But you have taken my dear one nearer to
yourself, and I tell myself that you know best and that
you act only in love and wisdom, even if it is beyond my
understanding.

I miss the presence of my dear one, the human ways, the
lovely qualities, even the little peculiarities, those things
that made . . . so different from anyone else.

O God, with whom there is no death, strengthen my
hope. Make me trust in eternal life, in eternal love.

I thank you for the life which has reached its earthly end,
which was so good, kind and helpful. Help me to be better
and to do better, because . . . lived. Give me courage
to carry on in the way of life, even as my
beloved will do for ever.
Amen
. . . .

Lord, we know that it is not your will that we should be
anxious, but we often are. We worry about so many
things. Help us to leave our worries with you because we
know that you care for us. Give us your peace, dear Lord.

I'm frightened, Lord. I've done something wrong and I'm
frightened of what will happen now. Forgive me and give
me courage to try and put it right – now, while I feel
sorry. Don't let me hide from it, justify it, or blame
others.

O God, give me the patience that I know I must have. Make me a little better every day until, bit by bit, I can shoulder the tasks of life again.

The prophet said: They who wait for the Lord shall renew their strength.

WILLIAM BARCLAY

. . . .

Lord, make me an instrument of your peace; where there is hatred let me sow love; where there is injury, pardon; where there is doubt, faith; where there is despair, hope; where there is darkness, light; and where there is sadness, joy.

. . . .

O Divine Master, grant that I may not so much seek to be consoled as to console; to be understood, as to understand; to be loved as to love; for it is in giving that we receive, it is in pardoning that we are pardoned and it is in dying, that we are born to eternal life.

SAINT FRANCIS OF ASSISI

❦ THE ❦

BIBLE SAYS

The Bible can speak to us on all occasions. In our hour of
darkness we can gain comfort and courage from it. The
following pages contain a selection of passages which,
you will find, reflect and express in an amazing way your
deepest thoughts and feelings. In a prayerful mood, may
they help you to find strength in your time of need.

The Twenty-third Psalm

The Lord is my shepherd; I shall not want.
He maketh me to lie down in green pastures: He leadeth
me beside the still waters.
He restoreth my soul.
He guideth me in the paths of righteousness for his
name's sake.
Yea, though I walk through the valley of the shadow of
death,
I will fear no evil; for thou art with me.
Thou prepareth a table before me in the presence of mine
enemies:
Thou anointeth my head with oil; my cup runneth over.
Surely goodness and mercy shall follow me all the days of
my life:
And I shall dwell in the house of the Lord for ever.

The Will of God

And he said: It is the Lord, let him do what seemeth him good.

. . . .

The Lord is nigh unto them that are of a broken heart; and saveth such as be of a contrite spirit.

. . . .

What? Shall we receive good at the hand of God, and shall we not receive evil?

. . . .

Wait on the Lord, be of good courage, and he shall strengthen thine heart; wait, I say, on the Lord.

. . . .

For I know my Redeemer liveth.

The voice of God

Fear not, I will help thee.

. . . .

Fear thou not, for I am with thee; be not dismayed, for I am thy God: I will strengthen thee, yea, I will help thee; yea, I will uphold thee with the right hand of my righteousness.

. . . .

As one whom his mother comforteth, so will I comfort you.

. . . .

If thou faint in the day of adversity, thy strength is small.

. . . .

Have I not commanded thee? Be strong and of good courage; be not afraid, neither be thou dismayed: for the Lord thy God is with thee withersoever thou goest.

From beyond the veil

I laid me down and slept; I awaked for the Lord sustained me.

. . . .

The Lord is my light and my salvation, whom then shall I fear? The Lord is the strength of my life: of whom then shall I be afraid?

. . . .

I will both lay me down in peace and sleep; for thou, Lord, only maketh me dwell in safety.

. . . .

Thou wilt show me the path of life; in thy presence is fullness of joy.

. . . .

Behold God is my salvation; I will trust and not be afraid: for the Lord God is my strength and my song; he also is become my salvation.

To our beloved

The sun shall be no more thy light by day; neither for brightness shall the moon give light unto thee: but the Lord shall be unto thee an everlasting light, and thy God thy glory.

. . . .

The Lord is thy keeper. The Lord shall preserve thee from all evil; he shall preserve thy soul. The Lord shall preserve thy going out and thy coming in from this time forth and for evermore.

. . . .

The souls of the righteous are in the hand of God,
And no hurt shall befall them.
...They are at peace,
And their hope is full of immortality.

. . . .

Thy sun shall no more go down; neither shall thy moon withdraw itself; for the Lord shall be thine everlasting light, and the days of thy mourning shall be ended.

. . . .

Wither thou goest, I will go; and where thou lodgest, I will lodge: thy people shall be my people, and thy God, my God. Where thou diest, will I die, and there I will be buried.

The memory of the just is blessed

And the spirit of the Lord rested upon him, the spirit of wisdom and understanding, the spirit of counsel and might, the spirit of knowledge and the fear of God.

. . . .

The law of truth was in his mouth, and iniquity was not found in his lips: he walked with me in peace and equity and did turn many away from iniquity.

. . . .

For the troubled

The vale of Trouble
A door of Hope.

. . . .

So teach us to number our days, that we may get us a heart of widsom.

. . . .

In quietness ... shall be your strength.

. . . .

God has said: I will never fail you, nor forsake you.